365 RANDOM AWESOME NUMBER FACTS

AMAZE & ANNOY OTHERS WITH CURIOUS NUMBER KNOWLEDGE

A Year's Worth of Awesome Number Facts

This book belongs to

_____

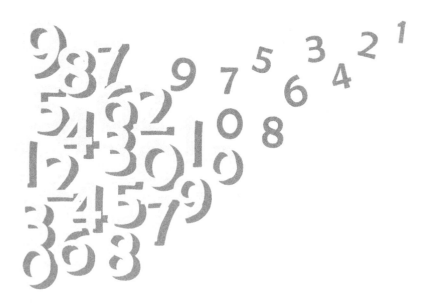

Think! Question! Imagine! GET CURIOUS!
Start a conversation!

Numbers are everywhere. They are all around us, connected to everything we do. Numbers help us measure, count, compare, see patterns, send information, locate things and people, determine time, distance, speed, imagine, understand concepts, invent, and create!

Inside this book you will find random awesome number facts that will change the way you think about the world, space, your body and mind, plus the randomness of the facts encourages curiosity! A single random fact could lead you on a surprising fact finding adventure.

Discover how many Earths could fit inside the Sun, the new height of Mt Everest, the average speed of a garden snail, the lean angle of the Leaning Tower of Pisa, the ratio of the perfect sugar cookie, how many jiffy's in a second, how long it would take you to count to a billion, and so much more.

Random number facts encourage curiosity, asking questions, problem solving, new ideas and EXPANDS THINKING!! Random Awesome Number Facts will Supercharge Your Mind.

That's the SUPER SUPERPOWER of NUMBER FACTS!

Everything around you is numbers.

Shakuntala Devi

1.

All insects have 6 legs.

2.

Every second your body produces
25 million new cells.

3.

Zero is an even number.

4.

Giraffes have the same number of
teeth as adult humans - 32.

5.

The creature with the most legs in the world is
a millipede found in Australia with 1300 legs.

6.

A googolplex is a number so large it has more zeroes that atoms in the universe. There are too many 0's to write the number so it is represented as 10 to the power of google - 10^{google}

7.

A garden snail has around 14,000 teeth.

8.

If you smoothed out all the wrinkles in your brain it would lay flat and be about the size of a standard pillowcase (52 x 66 cm/ 20x26 in).

9.

Less than 2% of people have red hair.

10.

You produce around 21,000 litres of spit in a lifetime. That's enough spit to fill 210 bathtubs with 100 litres of spit each.

11.

As at 2021 the number of people who have been to space is over 600.

12.

The number of hairs on your head depends on the colour of your hair. People with naturally blonde hair have 41% more hair follicles and hair than people with red hair, 24% than people with brown hair and 31% than people with black hair.

13.

71% of the Earth's surface is water.

14.

Only 3% of Earth's water is freshwater.

15.

Cats have 230 bones in their body.

16.

There are currently around 22 billion devices connected to the internet.

17.

There are 96 bags of human waste on the Moon left behind by astronauts of 6 Apollo missions.

18.

The average person farts between 5-15 times a day.

19.

The average football (soccer) player runs 15.3 km (9.5 miles) in a single match.

20.

You blink around 20 times a minute.

21.

Humans have 2 more chromosomes than a potato.

22.

Humans share 70% of our DNA with slugs.

23.

In camera terms the human eye is 576 megapixels.

24.

The fastest insect is the dragonfly. It can reach speeds up to 56 km/h (34.8 mph).

25.

The average sized man eats around 33 tonnes of food over a lifetime, which is around the weight of six African elephants.

26.

A cow can have around 40,000 jaw movements a day

27.

The radio took 38 years to reach an audience of 50 million. The iPod took 3 years to reach the same milestone.

28.

The first product to be scanned with a barcode was a packet of chewing gum in 1974.

29.

It is estimated that humans have around 60,000 thoughts a day, 90% of them are repetative.

30.

Insects outnumber humans around 200 million to 1.

31.

Jellyfish have survived more than 500 million years despite having no brains.

32.

The average shower lasts 8 minutes. The shower time recommended to save water is 4 minutes.

33.

The average depth of the ocean is 3.7 kms (2.3 miles).

34.

Your tongue is covered in around 8000 tastes buds.

35.

World Statistic Day is 20th of October every fifth year. It was created by the United Nations to celebrate statistics and all the important things they tell us.

36.

The sun is around 1,000,000
(a million) times bigger than Earth.

37.

1,300,000 Earths could fit

inside the sun.

38.

UY Scuti is the largest star currently known

in the universe. Almost 5 billion suns could

fit inside UY Scuti.

39.

A 1-minute kiss can burn 26 calories.

40.

If you could fly a commercial plane to Pluto

the trip would take around 680 years.

41.

The fear of the number 13 is called triskaidekaphobia.

42.

The most times a person has been stung by a bee without dying is 2,443.

43.

Only 13 people have been to the deepest part of the ocean, Challenger Deep in the Mariana Trench.

44.

The word 'hundred' comes from the old Norse term 'hundrath' which means 120 and not 100.

45.

Over 6000 people have reached the summit of Mount Everest the world's hightest mountain.

46.

Isosceles triangles have legs. The 2 equal length sides of an isosceles triangle are known as 'legs'.

47.

There are thirteen letters in the word sums 'eleven plus two' and 'twelve plus one' and the answer is 13.

48.

Mount Everest weighs an estimated 357 trillion pounds.

49.

'A jiffy' is one trillionth of a second.

50.

The mathematical ratio for the perfect sugar cookie is 3:2:1.

3 parts flour, 2 parts butter, 1 part sugar.

51.

In America there is roughly
1 convienience store for ever 2,245 people.

52.

The numbers of the opposite side of a dice
always add up to 7.

53.

My Very Excited Mother Just Sent Us Nachos
is a pattern of letters to help remember the
7 planets from Mercury to Neptune.
(Mercury Venus Earth Mars Jupiter Saturn Neptune)

54.

Nearly 80% of oxygen on Earth is produced
by underwater plants and aquatic life.

55.

The human brain is 78% water.

56.

The record for the world's oldest person belongs to French woman Jeanne Clament. She lived for 122 years and 164 days.

57.

Hand and palm are old measuring units.
1 hand = 10.16 cm (4 inches)
1 palm = 7.62 cm (3 inches)

58.

Every year 98 % of the atoms in the human body are replaced.

59.

All your blinking in one day = having your eyes closed for around 30 minutes.

60.

People spend on average 4.5 hrs a day on a mobile device.

61.

According to a study of over 6 million police records, crime peaks at 18 degrees Celsius in Manchester, England.

62.

The record for the longest professional tennis match lasted 11 hours and 5 minutes. It was played over 3 days between John Isner and Nicolas Mahit at Wimbledon in 2010.

63.

1 drop pf water contains around
470 quintillion molecules.
That's 470 followed by 18 zero's
470, 000, 000, 000, 000, 000, 000.

64.

If you add up all the numbers from 1-100 consecutively (1+2+3+4+5+6...) the total = 5050.

65.

When lightning strikes Earth it can reach temperatures 5x hotter than the surface of the sun.

66.

Farmed chickens today are 364% bigger than chickens 50 years ago.

67.

Houseflies beat their wings about 345 times a second.

68.

Lightning strikes Earth 6,000 times every minute.

69.

90% of Earth's population live in the Northern Hemisphere.

70.

Walking can boost creativity by up to 60%.

71.

The longest recorded flight of a chicken was 13 seconds.

72.

The average person will yawn around 250,000 times during their life.

73.

There are more atoms in 1 glass of water than glasses of water in all the oceans on Earth.

74.

On average 200-400 tracked objects enter Earth's atmosphere every year - almost a piece of space junk everyday.

75.

The total mass of all space objects floating around Earth's orbit is more than 9,900 tonnes. (including a spanner dropped from the International Space Station.)

76.

There are around twice as many kangaroos in Australia than there are people.

77.

10 human body parts have names 3 letters long – eye, hip, arm, leg, ear, toe, jaw, rib, lip, gum.

78.

There are over 2.5 million rivets in the Eiffel Tower.

79.

It takes around 3 million presses to wear down a button on an Xbox controller.

80.

There were 3 million rivets in the Titanic.

81.

There are over 6 million rivets in the Sydney Harbour Bridge in Australia.

82.

Mosquitoes can drink up to 3 x their body weight in blood.

83.

It would take 1.2 million mosquitoes, each sucking at once to completely drain the blood of an average human.

84.

Cats spend 66% of their life asleep.

85.

8% of people have an extra rib.

86.

If you multiply 1089 x 9 you get 9801 – that is the number 1089 reversed.

87.

Up to 30 trillion red blood cells pass through your heart in 1 minute.

88.

Over a lifetime of 80 years your heart will pump around 200 million litres (53 million gallons) of blood around your body. That's enough blood to fill an oil tanker.

89.

In 1 day, an adult heart pumps enough blood to fill around 39 bathtubs.

90.

An Australian red kangaroo can cover 7.5 metres in one hop.

91.

It would take around 533,333 red kangaroo hops to cross Australia.

92.

95% of the ocean is unexplored.

93.

Scientists believe there are over 2 million undiscovered animal species in the ocean.

94.

Saturn takes 29 years to orbit the sun.

95.

The longest hot dog ever made was 203.8 metres (1,996 feet).

96.

There are 28 bones on the human adult skull – 8 cranial, 14 facial and 6 ear bones.

97.

In 2000 table tennis balls were enlarged from 38mm to 40 mm. The increase in size was to slow the ball down, increase the rally time between competitors and help make it a more enjoyable spectator sport.

98.

A sloth can take up to 30 days to digest a meal.

99.

Mozart lived for 35 years and wrote 41 symphonies.

100.

A sheep dog can smell 44 times better than a human.

101.

Humans have 5 million olfactory cells in our noses, sheep dogs have 220 million.

102.

45 is the number of balls used in most lottery draws around the world. The odds of having 6 winning numbers from 45 balls is 1 in 8,145,060. (around 1 in 8.1 million)

103.

A human spends around 3 months of life on the toilet.

104.

There are 54 stickers on a Rubik's cube.

105.

There are over 43 quintillion Rubik's Cube combinations -

43,252,003,274,489,856,000 colour configurations and only 1 solution.

106.

The body of an average adult human weighing 70 kg contains among many things -

45 litres of water.

Around the same about of phosphorus as 220 match heads.

Enough iron to make a 7.5cm (3 inch) nail.

Enough lime to whitewash 1 small shed.

Enough fat to make 7 bars of soap.

0.2 milligrams of gold.

107.

Humans are born with 300 bones but some bones fuse together as we grow older.

108.

By the time you become and adult you have 206 bones in your body.

28 in your skull

1 horseshoe shaped. Bone in your neck

26 vertebrae

52 feet bones (26 in each foot)

24 ribs

1 collar bone

3 pelvis (the pelvis is made up of 3 bones)

6 arm bones (3 in each arm)

8 leg bones (4 in each leg)

54 hand bones (27 in each hand)

1 breastbone (sternum)

2 shoulder bones (scapula)

109.

During a lifetime a person's skin will be replaced around 900 times.

110.

The ten oldest people to ever live were women.

111.

The average British person will consume around 7,560 chocolate bars, 2,268 slices of chocolate cake and 8,316 chocolate biscuits in a lifetime.

112.

The average American will spend almost $30,000 US on snacks in a lifetime.

113.

Chocolate is the number 1 snack in the world.

114.

The average person will spend a total of 3680 hours or 153 days of their life searching for misplaced items.

115.

It would take you around 30 years to count to 1 billion.

116.

Humans make up less than ½ of all internet traffic. Over 60% of internet traffic comes from non-human use (bots & hacking tools).

117.

There are about three hundred thousand billion billion jiffys in a second.

118.

In summer the Antarctic is home to
45 species of birds.

119.

The genetic similarity between a
human and a banana is 60%.

120.

A dog has between 319-321 bones in total.
Dogs with longer tails have 2 extra tail bones.

121.

Earth travels through space at nearly
30 kilometres per second (67,000miles an hr).

122.

A jellyfish is 95% water.

123.

The average human belly button contains around 67 different types of bacteria.

124.

Humans carry around 100 trillion microorganisms in their intestines.

125.

The furthest recorded flight by a paper plane made from a single sheet of A4 paper is 69.14 meters (226 feet 10 inches).

126.

The longest game of Monopoly on record lasted 70 days.

127.

The human body has around 73 kilometres of nerves (45.36 miles).

128.

Google handles around 8.5 billion searches a day.

129.

The largest whale, the blue whale has 356 bones, and their lower jawbone is the largest bone on Earth.

130.

The current title of -
World's Smallest Known Animal
With A Backbone,
goes to a tiny frog that only grows to around the size of a housefly found in Papua New Guinea and averages only 7.7millimetres in length.

131.

The animal with the largest mouth is the bowhead whale. Its mouth can be as long as 4.9metres (16 feet) 3.7m high (12 feet) and 2.4m wide (8 feet). I also has a tongue that can weigh up to 907kg (1 ton).

132.

The temperature of the Moon varies between 106 degrees Celsius during the day (224 degrees Fahrenheit) to -183 degrees Celsius at night (-298 degrees Fahrenheit).

133.

A giraffe has 208 bones - 2 more bones than an adult human.

134.

Most golf balls have between 300-500 dimples.

135.

Most people burp between 6-20 times a day.

136.

There are over 1000 different species of bats in the world. A bat can eat up to 3000 insects in a night.

137.

Humans are 30 times more likely to laugh around other people.

138.

Australia has the greatest number of reptiles in the world – over 750 species.

139.

10-15 minutes of laughing can burn up to 40 calories.

140.

You can cut a pie into 8 pieces in three cuts.

141.

Queen ants can live for decades. Male ants live little more than a week.

142.

4 babies are born every second.

143.

Archaeologists believe the construction of Stonehenge took around 1500 years.

144.

The tallest building in the world, Burj Khalifqin in Dubai, is 828 metres tall with 163 floors. It took six years to build.

145.

In America the most popular month to be born is September with September 9 being the most popular day.

146.

On average a person will spend 25 years asleep over a lifetime.

147.

It would take only 1 hour to drive to space if you could drive straight up in the air.

148.

There are 41,806 languages spoken in the world today.

149.

There are more than 10 million bricks in the Empire State Building.

150.

There are over 900 million km's (550 million miles) of undersea internet cables that carry data across the world in a fraction of a second.

151.

The 24-hour day comes from the Ancient Egyptians. They designed a system of splitting night & day into two sets of 12 hours.

152.

The most common slope angles which avalanches occur is between 36-38 degrees.

153.

In ten seconds over 30 million emails will have been sent worldwide.

154.

In 1 minute there are 3.8 million searches on Google.

155.

The average person spends 6 hours and 57 minutes looking at a screen everyday.

156.

The tallest person ever was Robert Wadlow (1918-1940) from the USA. He was 2.72 metres tall (8ft 11in.)

157.

11 is the number of players on a side in football, soccer, cricket, and field hockey.

158.

There are round 6-10 million different species of insects.

159.

The record for the widest mouth belongs to Francisco Joaquim (born 1990) from Angola. His mouth is 17cm (6.69in) wide.

160.

15 minutes of laughter a day can help you burn between 10-40 calories.

161.

If you travelled at the speed of light for 1 second you would cover 299,792 kms (186,292 miles).

162.

Travelling at light speed you could circle Earth 7 times in one second.

163.

Brushing your teeth for 3 minutes burns 10 calories.

164.

Mars has lower gravity than Earth. A person weighing 90 kg (200 pounds) on Earth would only weigh 34.5 kg (76 pounds) on Mars.

165.

You are shorter at night than in the morning.

166.

A dolphin can hear sounds up to 24 km (15 miles) away.

167.

Humpback whale songs can travel through water over 16,000 kms (10,000 miles).

168.

Only male humpback whales sing. They are known to sing for up to 20 minutes .

169.

The average lead pencil can be used to draw a line 56 km long (35 miles) or to write approximately 50,000 English words.

170.

80% of babies are born with birthmarks but most fade away over time.

171.

In one study, 70% of people tilted their heads to the right rather than the left when kissing someone.

172.

The average person will say around 7000 words a day.

173.

Only one in every 2 billion people will live to be 116 years old.

175.

Every 10 years the human skeleton repairs and renews itself.

176.

1 in every 2000 babies already has a tooth when they are born.

177.

Every 10 days human taste buds get replaced.

178.

The record for the longest it has rained without stopping is 881 days at Honomu Maki, Oahu Hawaii from 1913-1916.

179.

In the average lifetime it is estimated a person will breathe in around 20 kg(44lb) of dust.

180.

Your little finger is responsible for 50% of your hand strength.

181.

Humans can recognise a sound in as little as 0.05 seconds, which is less time than it takes to blink.

182.

Your big toe bears 40% or your body weight.

183.

On average your body takes 12 hours to digest food.

184.

Your sense of smell is on average
100x stronger than your sense of taste.

185.

Outer space officially begins
100 kms (62 miles)
above sea level .

186.

US park ranger Roy Sullivan was struck
by lightning 7 times in his life and
survived all 7 strikes.

187.

The record for the largest number of
kittens in the same cat litter is 19.

188.

Most people can only remember a sequence of 7 numbers correctly.

189.

In 2015 Chao Lu of China accurately recited 67,890 numbers of pi from memory.

190.

The record for the longest cat tail measured and recorded is 44.66cm (17.58inches).

191.

A lunar cycle is 29.5 days.

It talks 254 to complete 12 full moons. As this is shorter than a calendar year of 365 days, roughly every 2.5 years there is a 13th moon in the calendar year.

192.

Cats have one more eyelid than humans.

The 3rd eyelid acts like a windshield wiper.

193.

Studies suggest that children ask around

73 questions every day.

194.

Standing around doing nothing

can burn 75-100 calories.

195.

The average speed of a garden snail is

0.048km/hr (0.013m/s).

196.

75% of the world's diet is produced from

12 plant and 5 animal species.

197.

A sneeze can travel 4.5 meters second.

(10 miles/hr)

198.

The temperature of the Earth's core is
around 7,500 Kelvin,
which is hotter than the surface of the sun.

199.

Mercury and Venus are the only 2 planets in
our solar system that do not have a moon.

200.

The bumblebee bat is the world's smallest
bat and the world's smallest mammal.
They only grow to 29-33mm in length (1.1-1.3
inches). This is around the size of a large
bumblebee.

201.

Saturn has 82 moons.

202.

Australia has over 10,000 beaches. You could visit a new beach everyday for 27 years.

203.

The bumblebee bat is only found in 2 countries – Thailand and Myanmar.

204.

On average the tooth fairy currently pays $5.36 per visit. According to a poll, the rate for a tooth purchased by the tooth fairy has increased 14% since 1998.

205.

Surgeons who play video games for at least 3 hours a week perform 27% faster and make 37% fewer mistakes.

206.

37% of video game players said racing is their most played genre.

206.

In 2022 there were 126 million active Minecraft players.

207.

Up to 54% of boys 3-12 play Minecraft and 32% of girls.
32% of boys also watch Minecraft related content on YouTube.

208.

Google rents 200 goats to eat the grass surrounding their headquarters in Mountain View California. The goats usually take a week to eat the grass and they fertilize the grass at the same time.

209.

The Milky Way Galaxy is 18,105,700 light years wide.

210.

A day on planet Mars is 24 hours 39 minutes and 35 seconds long.

211.

There are more than 1,600 major volcanoes on planet Venus, though most are long extinct and currently not erupting.

212.

There are approximately 2 trillion galaxies in the observable universe.

213.

A day on Pluto is 153.6 hours long.

That's 6.4 Earth days!

(6 days, 9 hours and 36 mins to be more exact)

214.

Only 5% of the universe is visible from Earth.

215.

Light travels from the Sun to Earth in less than 10 minutes.

217.

Wildlife technician Richard Thomas took the tongue twister 'how much wood would a woodchuck chuck if a woodchuck could chuck wood?', and calculated a rough estimate to be 317kg (700pounds).

218.

The International Space Station circles Earth every 92 minutes.

219.

In 24 hours the International Space Station orbits Earth 16 times.

220.

Children have more taste buds than adults. Infants have around 30,000 taste buds. Children have around 10,000 older adults have 5,000.

221.

The first ever black hole photographed is 3 million times the size of Earth.

222.

Mars has less than 1% of Earth's atmosphere.

223.

The moon is moving away from Earth at a rate of 4cm a year (1.6 inches)

224.

Earth weighs 81 times more than the moon.

225.

1 day on Mercury = 58 Earth days.

226.

On average it takes light 1.3 seconds to travel from Moon to Earth.

227.

The distance between Earth and Moon is 384,400 kms (238,855 miles).

228.

It takes about 3 days for a spacecraft
with astronauts to reach the moon.

229.

A toss of a coin is not a 50:50 chance.
If the coin is tossed heads up,
it is more likely to land on heads.

230.

The ratio for a coin toss is
51% heads and 49% tails.

231.

People spend around 13% of their life
'zoned out',thinking of nothing.

232.

Halley's comet will pass over
Earth again on July 26 2061.

233.

There is a spacecraft graveyard in the Southern Pacific Ocean known as 'Point Nemo.' It has over 300 pieces of space debris.

234.

The Antarctic Polar Desert is the world's largest desert. It covers roughly 14 million square kilometres (5.4 million square miles).

235.

40 million years ago gigantic penguins around 180 cm tall (6ft), taller than most adults, lived in the Antarctic Peninsula.

236.

In 1783 a volcanic eruption in South Iceland killed 80% of the world's sheep.

237.

The Eiffel Tower grows in the summer. Due to heat expansion of the towers iron, it can gain up to 15cm (6 inches) in height.

238.

The letter E is the most common letter in the English alphabet.The letter 'E' appears in roughly 11% of all English words.

239.

Greenland sharks can live up to 500 years old.

240.

You are more likely to be struck by lightning than bitten by a shark.
Odds of being struck by lightning in a given year, 1 in 1.6 million.
Odds of being bitten by a shark in a given year, 1 in 3.7 million.

241.

Odds of finding a 4 leaf clover on your first try is 1 in 5000.

242.

In 2013 thieves stole 5 tonnes of Nutella from a truck trailer in Germany.
That's equivalent to 6,875 jars of Nutella.

243.

Cheese is the most stolen food in the world.
It is estimated that 4% of the world's cheese ends up stolen.

245.

A nibble is a quantity of data.
1 nibble = 4 bits.

244.

Cucumber is 96% water.

245.

Cows can poo up to 15 times a day.

246.

It is estimated if all the people on Earth jumped at the same time a earthquake between 4-8 magnitude could be produced.

247.

Caterpillars have about 4,000 muscles. People have 629.

248.

A shake is a unit of time measurement. 1 shake = 10 nanoseconds.

249.

The term "two shakes of a lambs' tail," means 20 nanoseconds.

250.

It takes 6-8 minutes to hard boil an egg.

251.

A flea can jump 350 x its own body length. This is the equivalent to a human jumping a football field.

252.

Ostrich eggs are the largest of all eggs. 1 ostrich egg is about 24 x the size of 1 chicken egg.

253.

1 ostrich egg can weigh around 20 x more than 1 chicken egg.

254.

A bakers dozen is 13.

255.

A wiffle is a unit of measure used by marine biologists to measure coral.
1 wiffle = 8.90 cm (3.5 inches)

256.

You would not be able to count the number of nerve cells in the human brain in one lifetime. Scientists say it would take over 3000 years to count.

257.

One horse length is approximately 2.4 meters (8 feet).

258.

The blue whale has the biggest heart on Earth, weighing around 180kg (400 pounds). When they dive deep for food it can slow to only beating 2 x per minute.

259.

Watermelon is 92% water.

260.

The number 1 most eaten food in the world is eggs.

number 2 = rice

number 3 = chicken

261.

The world generates 10x more trash today than it did 100 years ago.

262.

Football (soccer) is the most popular sport
in the world with over 4 billion followers.
That's more than half the population of Earth.

263.

Snickers candy bar is the number 1 bestselling
candy bar in the world.
Over 2 billion bars are sold every year.

264.

Every insect is a host to around 10
bacterial species.

265.

Scientists have discovered the remains of a
100-million-year-old baby snake inside a
piece of amber from Myanmar. The snake
lived before T-Rex walked the Earth.

266.

Caterpillars have 6 eyes.

267.

The average lifespan of a
butterfly is 2-4 weeks.

268.

The average lifespan of a
cockroach is 20-30 weeks.

269.

The average lifespan of a
housefly is 15-30 days.

270.

The female chaco golden knee tarantula
spider can live for 20-30 years.

271.

There are over 5000 species of ladybugs.

272.

The Dead Sea has 8 - 9 times more salt than other oceans and seas of the world.

273.

To make 450 grams (one pound) of honey, a hive of bees must visit around 2 million flowers.

274.

A 'bit' is the smallest unit of storage information.

8 bits = 1 byte

275.

A yottabyte is unit of data storage so large it is for computers of the future.
4 yottabytes is 250,000 times the entire digital memory on Earth today.

276.

An adult brain weighs 1.36kgs (3 pounds)

277.

An infant brain weighs 400 grams (14.1 ounces)

278.

A sperm whales' brain is the largest on Earth.
It is five times heavier than a human brain.
It can weigh up to 7-9 kgs (20 pounds).

279.

A ragworms brain is the smallest on Earth measuring 17-180 micrometres.

(Ragworms are cousins of the earthworm).

280.

A human brain uses
20% of the body's oxygen.

281.

Human cells only make up 43% of the body's total cell count, the rest belong to microscopic organisms known as out microbiome.

282.

On average a person takes
16 breaths per minute.

283.

Most starfish have 5 arms called rays.
If a starfish has more than 5 rays it will often
have rays in multiples of 5. There could be
10, 15,20 even 30 rays on one starfish. This is
called five-fold symmetry.

284.

The number of segments in an orange is
usually 10 but can range from 9-12.

285.

Most lemons have 8-9 segments.

286.

The lifespan of a walrus is around 40 years.

287.

A hexagon is a shape with 6 sides of equal length. Some of the places you find a hexagon in nature are bee honeycomb, snowflakes and on tortoise shells.

288.

The hexagon is one of the most common shapes found in nature.

289.

Humans have 5 vital organs - heart, lungs, kidneys, liver, brain. Without any of these you will not survive.

290.

In a lifetime, on average a person walks 160,934 kms (100,000 miles).

291.

It is rare for a person to have two equally sized feet. One foot is almost always larger.

292.

There are approximately 250,000 sweat glands in a persons feet.
(125,000 each foot).

293.

An adult human circulates about 5.6 litres of blood through the body
three times every minute.

294.

By the time a human is 70yrs they would have consumed around 54,553 litres
(12,000 gallons) of water.

295.

Every 4-5 days the lining of the human stomach replaces itself.

296.

The lifespan of a human eyebrow hair is on average 4 months.

297.

The human muscular system consists of over 650 muscles.
You use 22 muscles to swivel your head.

298.

You use 9 muscles to pick up a cup.

299.

You use around 100 muscles to speak.

300.

You use 17 muscles to cry.

301.

You use 38 muscles to send a text.

302.

You use 35 muscles to kiss.

303.

It is impossible to only use 1 muscle.

304.

It takes 155 muscles to cycle.

305.

The human face used 43 muscles
to express facial emotion.

306.

It is estimated that humans can make
around 10,000 facial expressions.

307.

A smile uses 12 muscles.

A frown uses 11 muscles.

308.

Humans lose an entire outer layer of skin
in around 2-4 weeks, roughly shedding
500 million cells a day.

309.

The 1 muscle that is only attached at one end is the tongue.

310.

A blink lasts on average 100-150 milliseconds.

311.

There is 20 billion kilometres of DNA in a human.

312.

0.062 cubic metres is the average physical space taken up by a human body.

313.

Humans have existed for less than 1% of human history.

314.

The oldest living tree in 2022 is 4852 yrs old.

315.

Earth is around 4.5 billion years old.

316.

99.9% of all life that has ever existed on Earth is now extinct.

317.

In the last 500 years it is estimated 900 species of animals have become extinct.

318.

The silk thread of a Chilean recluse spider is five times stronger than steel.

319.

A silk spider thread stretching around the world would only weigh 320grams.

320.

Dinosaurs became extinct around 66 million years ago.

321.

Dinosaurs existed for nearly 175 million years.

322.

450 people die annually in the USA from falling out of bed.

323.

Sharks have been swimming in the ocean for 450 million years.

324.

The Earth's diameter is 12,742 km (7,917.5 miles).

325.

Ants first appeared on Earth 140-168 million years ago.

326.

The Arctic tern is the bird that travels the farthest on Earth. Each year it can travel 40,000 kms (24,000 miles). Over a lifetime of 30 years it can fly 1 million kilometres (620,000 miles).

327.

Chickens currently outnumber humans on Earth almost 3:1

328.

There are more than 19 billion chickens on Earth.

329.

There are around 2 billion pigs on Earth.

330.

There are around 1.5 billion cows on Earth.

331.

As of 2020 it was estimated there were 102 men for every 100 women in the world.

332.

A wombat can sprint for 90 seconds at up to 40 km/hr (24.8mph)

333.

A heaviest watermelon ever recorded weighed 159kg (350 pounds).

334.

The heaviest pumpkin ever grown
weighed 1226kgs. (2,703 pounds)
That is around the same weight as
17.5 adult men, or one small car.

335.

Saltwater crocodiles are the world's oldest
and largest reptile. They can grow up to
7 metres long(23 feet) and weigh 1000kgs
(2205 pound).

336.

The Australian rocket frog can
leap 50 times its own body length.
That's around 2 metres (78 inches).

337.

1 light year is approximately
9.6 trillion kilometres
(5.88 trillion miles).

338.

Our nearest galaxy is Andromeda galaxy.
it is 2.3 million light years away.

339.

The Leaning Tower of Pisa currently leans
at an angle of 3.99 degrees.

340.

Scientists have estimated that the
maximum angle the Leaning Tower of Pisa
can lean before it falls is 5.44 degrees.

341.

The projected world population in 2100
is 11.2 billion.

342.

1 nanometer =1 billionth of a metre

343.

A human hair is approximately
80,000-100,000 nanometres wide.

344.

1 nanometre is about the size a human
fingernail grows in 1 second.

345.

1 strand of human DNA is
2.5 nanometres in diameter.

346.

You could fit Rhode Island into
Alaska 425 times.

347.

It would take over 181 million years to
download all the data on the internet.

348.

A zettabyte is a measurement
for large data storage.
1 zettabyte =1 billion terabytes
In 2022 it is estimated all the data on the
internet is around 44 zettabytes.
By 2025 it is expected the internet will be
175 zettabytes.

349.

A thunderstorm cloud can contain 1.1 million tons of water.

350.

In 2020 the height of Mt Everest was increased 0.86 metres to a new official height of 8,848.86m (29,032 ft).

351.

A dung beetle can pull 1.141 times its own body weight.

352.

There are over 32,000 species of fish in the world.

353.

The fastest land animal on earth is the cheetah which can reach speeds of 80-100 km/hr (49-80mph)

354.

The deepest cave in the world is Veryovkina Cave. It has a depth of 2212 metres (7257 feet).

355.

The fastest shark in the ocean is the shortfin mako. It can reach speeds up to 56 Km/hr (35mph).

356.

The fastest human swimmer swims around 9km/hr (6mph).

357.

The Pearl of Puerto is the largest known pearl in the world. It weighs 34 kilograms and has an estimated value of US$100 million.

358.

An adult human contains around 7 octillion atoms. That's 7 followed by 24 zeros, 7, 000, 000, 000, 000, 000, 000, 000, 000.

359.

A skin cell is about 30 micrometers across.

360.

There are 1.1 billion sheep on Earth.

361.

Cabbage is 91% water.

362.

There are 14 billion pencils made each year worldwide. The average size tree has enough wood to make 170,000 pencils.

363.

As much as 25 % of all the food we eat depends on pollination by honey bees.

364.

A single 30 metre tall mature tree can absorb more than 22 kilograms (50 pounds) of carbon dioxide a year and release enough oxygen per year back into the atmosphere to support a family of 4.

365.

On average, a small fluffy white cumulus cloud floating in the sky weighs 500,000 kilograms, which is roughly the weight of 100 African elephants.

CONGRATULATIONS!

365 AWESOME, RANDOM NUMBER FACTS KNOWLEDGE AWARD

to

Signed:

Date:

Look out for our other fun filled fact books!

Amaze! Surprise!Entertain! Annoy! Improve creativity! Start conversation!

Find out which country does not have mosquitoes, the number of muscles in a caterpillar, which city has its own ant, there to find the longest staircase in the world and much more!

QUICK RANDOM FUN FACTS
Loads of different topics - animals, history, science, maths, language, general knowledge ...
PLUS FUN TRIVIA QUESTIONS TO TEST YOUR KNOWLEDGE.

Does hot or cold water freeze faster?
What food will cockroaches not eat?
What causes belly button lint?
What is the strongest shape?
Plus so much more!

Don't forget to leave us a review so others can find our books too!
Thank you !

There is no such thing as useless knowledge. You never know what door it's going to open up for you.

Benjamin Carson

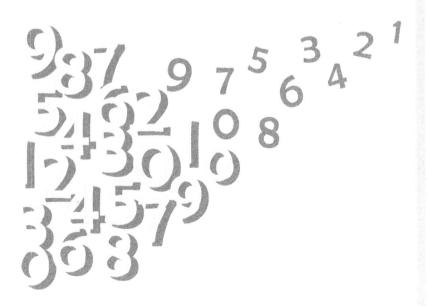

Record a day of random number facts :

Name: Date:

Age: Years: Days:

Time of day:

Postcode: latitude: longitude:

Number of steps taken in day:

Distance travelled:

Number of people spoken to:

Number of friends seen:

Number of hours sleeping:

Time spent school/work/home:

Total hours of screen time:

Time spent playing sport:

Number of text messages sent:

Number of clouds you can see right now:

Record your own RANDOM AWESOME NUMBER FACTS :

Record your own RANDOM AWESOME NUMBER FACTS :

Record your own RANDOM AWESOME NUMBER FACTS :

Printed in Great Britain
by Amazon

21314844R00058